Read and Do Science

SOUND

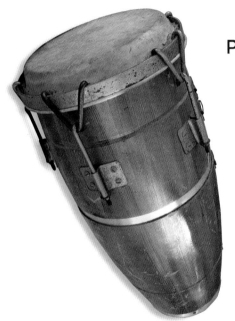

Written by Melinda Lilly
Photos by Scott M. Thompson
Design by Elizabeth Bender

Educational Consultants

Kimberly Weiner, Ed.D

Betty Carter, Ed.D

Maria Czech, Ph.D
California State University Northridge

Rourke
Publishing LLC
Vero Beach, Florida 32963

Before You Read This Book

Think about these facts:

1. Have you ever heard an echo? What do you think made the echo? Why don't we hear echoes all the time?

2. Think of a loud sound that you can make. What do you do to make a loud sound? What do you do to make a sound that is very quiet?

The experiments in this book should be undertaken with adult supervision.

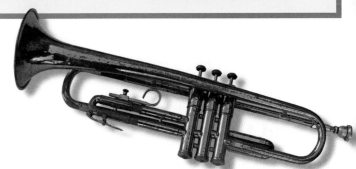

For Lance

—S. T.

www.rourkepublishing.com

Library of Congress Cataloging-in-Publication Data

ISBN 1-58952-644-9

Printed in the USA

Table of Contents

LISTEN UP!

This book is about sound,
but there's not much
to hear.

This is a book,
not a **tuba**.

4

Drop the book.

If you heard a thud when the book hit the floor, your ears did their job. They hear sounds.

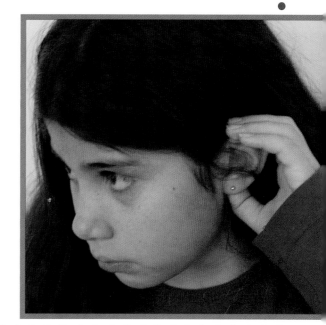

How did you hear the thud?

Sound wiggles through air like a **wave**.

These wiggles are called **vibrations**.

The Parts of the Ear That Vibrate

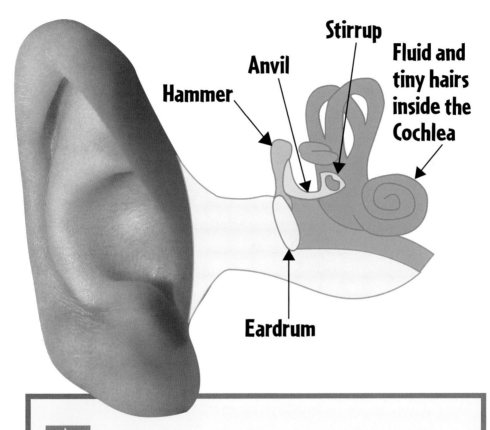

Hammer

Anvil

Stirrup

Fluid and tiny hairs inside the Cochlea

Eardrum

The sound wave made the inside of your ears shake, or **vibrate**. You heard the thud.

Sound gets quieter the farther it travels. Whisper to a friend far away. Can she hear you?

She can if you use a cup phone. It controls where sound travels.

Let's make a cup phone!

8

Cup Phone

What You Need:
- Two paper cups
- String
- Safety scissors
- Plastic butter knife

Use a plastic knife to make one slit in the bottom of each cup.

9

Hold a **spool** of string. Ask your friend to pull out the string as she walks away from you.

Whisper to each other. When you are too far away to hear the whispers, cut the string.

Poke an end of the string through the cup's slit.

Knot it.

Do the same to the other cup.

"Knot, knot"
"Who's there?"
"Knot."
"Knot who?"
"Knot me!

If you can't tie a knot, use tape.

You and your friend each take a cup. Walk away from each other until the string stretches tight.

Whisper into the cup. Why can you hear with the phone and not without?

Why Does the Cup Phone Work?

It traps the sound and sends it wiggling along the string to the other cup.

13

The Senses

Hearing is one of our **senses**. Senses help us experience the world. The other senses are sight, smell, taste, and touch. We can hear and feel sound.

A deaf child feels vibrations from a cello and signs the word, "Sound."

Feel sound tickle your mouth!

Buzz Flute

What You Need:
- Plastic straw
- Safety scissors
- Hole punch

Put one end of a straw in your mouth.

Bite down as you pull it out of your mouth. The end is now flattened.

ave an adult help you cut the corners off the flat end of the straw. It is now the shape of an alligator's mouth.

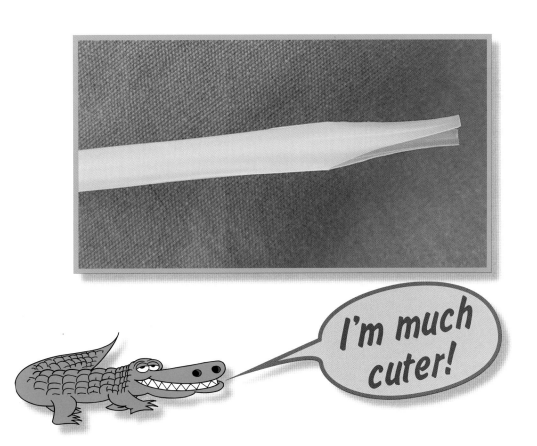

I'm much cuter!

Put the cut end all the way inside your mouth. Close your lips. Don't bite down. Blow hard. Do you hear and feel buzzing?

If it doesn't work, flatten the straw.

If it does work, we're sorry.

Why Does the Buzz Flute Work?

You blow air. The cut ends vibrate, making the buzzing sound.

Add holes to play different notes!

Slide the straw into a hole punch. Have an adult help you punch three holes along the straw.

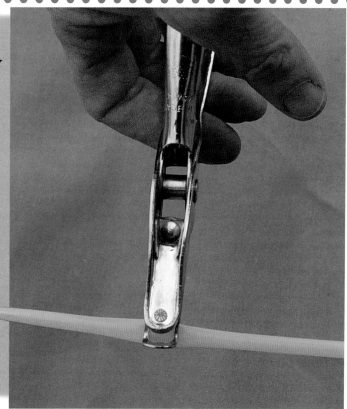

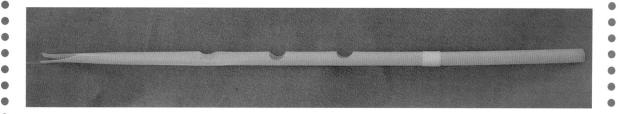

What happens to the sound when you cover up one hole? When all the holes are open?

● ●

Why Can You Play Different Notes?

When the holes are open, the sound vibrates quickly, making a high note. When you plug the holes, it takes longer for the blown air to leave the flute. The sound waves slow down. The note is lower.

What's the Buzz About Sound?

We can hear and feel it. Sound vibrates, moving in waves. The faster it vibrates, the higher the note. And sound can be soft or LOUD!

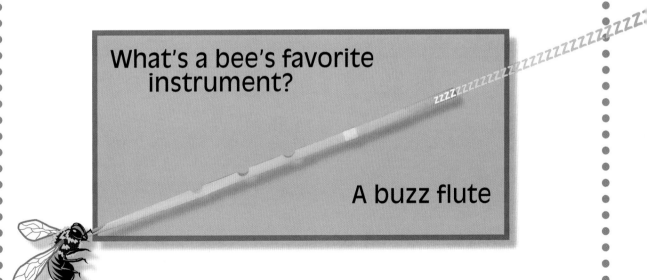

What's a bee's favorite instrument?

A buzz flute

Glossary

pluck (PLUK) — To quickly pull and let go of a string

senses (SEN suz) — Hearing, sight, taste, touch, and smell, the five senses are the powers that humans and animals use to become aware of the world and themselves

spool (SPOOL) — An object used for winding string

tuba (TOO buh) — A large wind instrument with a full, deep sound

vibrate (VY brayt) — To move quickly and evenly, quiver

vibrations (vy BRAY shunz) — Quick, even movements, tremors

wave (WAVE) — A curve or group of curves that follow one another in a forward movement

Take It Further: Cup Guitar

You and a friend put the cup phones to your ears. Stretch the string tight.

Pluck the string with your finger. What do you hear?

Have your friend run her hand along the string as you pluck.

How does the sound change? What makes the string vibrate quickly and play a high note?

Think About It!

1. Why do people cup a hand around each ear when they are trying to hear something more clearly? Why do people cup their hands around their mouth when they yell to someone far away?

2. Why are sounds quieter and fuzzier when you cover your ears?

3. If you want to pluck a high note on the sound guitar, should you shorten or lengthen the string? Why?

Index